soho
theatre company

Soho Theatre Company presents

MODERN DANCE FOR BEGINNERS

by **Sarah Phelps**

First performed at Soho Theatre on 23 September 2002

Performances in the Lorenz Auditorium

Soho Theatre is supported by

gettyimages

A&B
Arts & Business
NEW PARTNERS
Bloomberg
TBWA\GGT DIRECT

Registered Charity No: 267234

For my family

Thanks to everyone at Soho Theatre, to Elizabeth Freestone, to Paul Sirett for his continued support and encouragement and especially, thanks to my friends, for telling me to get on with it, for making me laugh, teaching me poker and keeping me sane. You all know who you are.

First published in 2002 by Oberon Books Ltd
521 Caledonian Road, London N7 9RH
Tel: +44 (0) 20 7607 3637 / Fax: +44 (0) 20 7607 3629
e-mail: info@oberonbooks.com
www.oberonbooks.com

A catalogue record for this book is available from the British Library.

ISBN: 978-1-84002-343-5

Cover photograph: Betsie Van der Meer/Getty Images

Characters

FRANCES
thirty-one
a bridesmaid and later a company strategist

OWEN
thirty-three
a bridegroom and later a too-ardent lover

JULIA
thirty-two
a spoiled daughter and betrayed wife

KIERAN
twenty-nine
a handy-man and jack-of-all-trades

RUSSELL
thirty-six
a failing media executive and terminal romantic

ELERI
twenty-two
an assistant sports shop manager

SKINNER
forty-four
a corporate reptile

LORRAINE
thirty-nine
a mother and oncologist

The action takes place over the course of a year.

The time is the present, the very recent past and variable futures.

All characters played by the same actor and actress. Changes in between scenes should be performed as part of the action, with the characters helping to dress and undress each other.

Scene 1

Summer. Late afternoon.

A hotel bedroom. Distantly, a party.

FRANCES, a bridesmaid. OWEN, a bridegroom. A light summer suit hangs on a hanger. Glasses, a bottle, perhaps.

FRANCES: Are you drunk?

OWEN: No. Not at all. Are you?

FRANCES: What do you think?

OWEN: You don't look it. So you are.

FRANCES: Yes, I am. 'Wankered' as your best man would say.

OWEN: Did you like him?

FRANCES: Not in the slightest. Why have I never met him before if he's such a good friend?

OWEN: Well, he's a new-ish sort of friend.

FRANCES: New friends for your new life.

OWEN: You didn't like him.

FRANCES: He's an arsehole. I can't believe that this is the man you chose to accompany you at the alter. You have so little faith in your future?

OWEN: What's that supposed to mean?

FRANCES: Well, you'd imagine that best man duties would fall to a good friend. A long term companion. If it's someone you only just met –

OWEN: I haven't only just met him –

FRANCES: Then the whole event, all this…excess, is a lot more disposable. Isn't it?

OWEN: I wanted him to do it. I thought he'd do a good job.

FRANCES: Perhaps a better friend would have told you that you didn't have to go through with it and we wouldn't be here now.

OWEN: I wanted to do this! Why can't you be happy for me?

FRANCES: Friend of Julia's, isn't he?

OWEN: Well, I met him through her but he's become a mate. A laugh.

FRANCES: Or I could have done it. I'd have done 'a good job'.

OWEN: You can't be a best man!

FRANCES: Better than being a bridesmaid. I could have been best woman. Seeing as how I am the best woman. I'd have made a great speech. I didn't recognise you from his speech. It was shit.

OWEN: Everyone was laughing.

FRANCES: They were just being polite. Now, I would have made a speech. Baby, I'd have brought the house down. Perhaps that's why you didn't ask me. You let that prick do it instead.

OWEN: I hoped you might get on. I described you to him.

FRANCES: How?

OWEN: Just...what you were like. You know, stuff. I showed him a photo. He was keen.

FRANCES: Don't do that to me, Owen. Just because he casts a shadow on a sunny day, don't try and palm me off on him! Jesus!

Beat.

'Was' keen. Not 'is'. But 'was'. You kept a photo of me?

OWEN: You shouldn't be here.

FRANCES: Where should I be?

OWEN: Mingling with guests.

FRANCES: Not a fucking chance.

OWEN: Helping Julia.

FRANCES: She's got plenty of help. Her 'extra specially close' girlfriends. They're all in there now, titivating over the 'going-away' outfit while Julia has a little rest. What does she need a rest for? It's not like she's been down the fucking mines! The 'extra specially close girlfriends' are all sitting with their feet up, gossiping about the good old days.

OWEN: You could join them.

FRANCES: They're not really my type.

OWEN: They're alright.

FRANCES: Spent much time with them, have you?

OWEN: Yes. Actually.

FRANCES: They all brush each other's hair and squeal. A lot. Adjust each other's earrings. Pull hems straight.

Ask each other if their breasts are symmetrical. Everything is so high-pitched and breathless.

OWEN: It's girl's talk. You do it.

FRANCES: They touch each other all the time. Have you noticed? Always making little excuses to touch each other. There's always some minute correction to be made that involves close personal contact. There's always a little mascara or lipstick smudge. It's very intimate. Rubbing their fingers round each others mouths. Caressing imaginary eyelashes off each other's cheeks. Not me, of course. They just about ignore me.

OWEN: They don't mean to. It's Julia's day. Come on.

FRANCES: And none of them smoke! How can you trust people who don't risk their lives forty times a day?

OWEN: You've cut down.

FRANCES: This morning, we're all back at the family manse, being tarted up and I was in the queue to get my hair and make-up done, went out and had a fag in the garden. The fuss! Doing this... (*She waves her hand in front of her face.*) and those little exaggerated coughs. And her, Queen Bitch, Ma fucking Baker, brings down a bottle of mouthwash and in front of everybody, that's everybody, suggests I might like to freshen my mouth before I have my make-up done. That's your mother-in-law. Good luck.

OWEN: I'm sure she didn't mean to hurt your feelings.

FRANCES: She didn't. In order for my feelings to be hurt, I'd have to give a toss. Then she asked me what I'd done with the butt. Said I just put it out and she

sent the maid, the *maid!* out into the garden with the
marigold gloves, with instructions to wrap the butt in
paper and put it in the dustbin.

OWEN: She's not a maid. She's their daily help.

FRANCES: There's a difference? The servant, then.
God. If I come again, I'm going to bring a crack pipe.
She is vile. The woman who put the cunt into the
country house. That hat! She looks like Roy Orbison
in drag.

OWEN: Cut them all some slack. They don't know you.
Join in a little. They're alright.

FRANCES: I can't stand being with them. All plucking
away at each other. You know what one of them,
Christ! What's her name? Very boring, really droopy
tits.

OWEN: Rowena.

FRANCES: Rowena! See, you knew who I meant!
Yes. Rowena said to me, as we were poised to enter
the bloody church, she turned and said 'Isn't this
exciting? It must be so wonderful for you!' Why for
me? Do I look like I've got a completely dismal life
and need Julia to gladden my existence? I could
become part of her little coterie. Pal up with turkey-
tits Rowena. Lucky, lucky me.

OWEN: Just because you haven't got any friends.

FRANCES: I think they're all lesbians. The way they
touch each other all the time. Sublimated Sapphic
desire.

OWEN: My bride's a lesbian? Things are really looking
up.

FRANCES: Well, they all met in the dorm at school, didn't they? I bet you that as soon as the lights went out they were in and out of each other's beds. All those cries and moans and tender endearments. One of the many benefits of a private education. You never get to see that kind of action in a comprehensive.

OWEN: Have you been taking drugs?

FRANCES: I hate them. Rowena and Cressy and Tavy and all their ilk. They're adults, grown up women and they still behave like they're in the dorm. It's like a cult. A cult of posh, inbred, repressed lesbians.

OWEN: They're not inbred!

FRANCES: Take a good look at their orbital ridges. Deformed. That's why they need you. Peasant stock. Add some much needed hybrid vigour to their piss-weak blood. Come the glorious day, citizen. I'll be there, packing some serious fire-power. No mercy. And yes, I've been snorting since 8.30 this morning. Columbian confetti.

OWEN: Fuck's sake!

FRANCES: Want a line?

OWEN: No.

FRANCES: You made her ask me to be a bridesmaid, didn't you?

OWEN: No. Julia wanted you. Of course she wanted you.

FRANCES: What about you?

OWEN: I should really think about getting ready.

FRANCES: I'm not stopping you.

OWEN: And who are you calling peasant stock?

FRANCES: You. Why don't you want to take your clothes off in front of me?

Beat.

OWEN: I've got this other suit to go away in.

FRANCES: Endless costume changes, isn't it? All dolled up like a dog's dinner. Very nice, though. Expensive. How does it feel to be rich?

OWEN: It crumples the minute you put it on.

FRANCES: Right.

OWEN: That's why I'm not getting changed now.

FRANCES: Right. If you say so.

OWEN: I'm pleased you're here.

FRANCES: Doesn't seem like it.

OWEN: Well, I am.

FRANCES: Why?

OWEN: I wanted to see you. Obviously. Find out how you are. So, how are you?

FRANCES: Oh, we're going to do this, are we? Social niceties?

OWEN: Why not? How have you been?

FRANCES: Fabulous.

OWEN: How's work?

FRANCES: Oh, shut up!

OWEN: I'm serious. I worry.

FRANCES: It's fine. We're being taken over. Rationalisation. Down-sizing. All that shit.

OWEN: You'll be alright though?

FRANCES: It's been me that's worked out the strategy. A fair few of my colleagues have their heads on the block and I'm responsible for putting them there. Madame Guillotine, that's me.

OWEN: How does that feel.

FRANCES: Great. Never liked them anyway. It won't happen for ages yet but when it does, I'm safe. On the up. For what it's worth.

OWEN: Seeing anyone?

FRANCES: Yes.

OWEN: Well, that's good. Does he have a name?

FRANCES: Russell.

OWEN: What do you call a man buried under leaves?

FRANCES does a 'punchline' drum roll, ending on imaginary cymbals.

FRANCES: Yeah, that'll be him.

OWEN: Is he nice?

FRANCES: I hope not.

OWEN: You could have brought him with you.

FRANCES: I didn't want to. He just fucks me. Your face.

OWEN: What about it?

FRANCES: That little crease between your eyebrows.
Frowning. You prude.

OWEN: I'm not a prude. I just don't like hearing you
talk about yourself like that.

FRANCES: It is what it is. He doesn't care. I don't care.
It's just fucking. What about you?

OWEN: We're not talking about me.

FRANCES: Do you love her?

OWEN: She's nice. A good person. She wanted us to
make up.

FRANCES: Didn't know we'd had an argument. You
didn't answer the question.

OWEN: Of course I do. Love her. Of course.

FRANCES: What's it like fucking her?

OWEN: I'm not answering that.

FRANCES: I told you about me –

OWEN: More details than I wanted –

FRANCES: That's because all you ever want to hear
is that everything's fine and there isn't going to be
any hassle or trouble and all of it's still waters, well
bollocks to you, Owen! Fucking idiot! Why can't you
answer the question! Do you like fucking her? Is it
good? Does she suck your cock without being asked?
Does she spit or swallow? Do you lose yourself?

OWEN: The way you talk...

FRANCES: Just answer the question!

OWEN: This is my wife!

FRANCES: Of four and a half hours.

OWEN: My bride!

FRANCES: Oh, I see, Julia's such an example of exalted womanhood, such a good nice person that you can't say or do any kind of fucking…

OWEN: Listen to you! If that's what you want… If that's all you want…to *reduce* yourself then, that's your choice but I don't want that, I want…

FRANCES: Do you 'make love' then? You and Julia? Is that what it is? No sweat and smells and noises. What does she do when she comes?

OWEN: It's none of your business!

FRANCES: Does she go 'Aaaah…' like a proper lady?

OWEN: Fuck you, Frances.

FRANCES: I'm starting to get the impression that you haven't gone anywhere near her yet. I bet you haven't been up her arse or anything impolite like that –

OWEN: We're very happy. I'm happy. I wanted this. I want it. I just don't want anyone to be unhappy. I don't want you to be unhappy.

FRANCES: Tough. When we were coming up the aisle, all I could see was the back of your head, waiting to plight your troth. That's all I could see. Like nothing else and no one else in there existed. You didn't look at me once.

OWEN: I knew you were there.

FRANCES: Not even during the photos. I was watching you. Talking and smiling with everyone else. But not me.

OWEN: I knew you were there. I didn't know how to be. What to say.

Pause.

FRANCES: These shoes pinch. They hurt.

OWEN: Take them off.

FRANCES: I'll never get them back on again. That's the thing with being of peasant stock. Broad feet, so we don't sink into the mud when we're picking stones out t'field for us tea. None of the other bridesmaids have shoes that pinch. That's breeding for you.

OWEN: If you're going to turn this into some stupid... class thing... Just take the bastard things off if they hurt that much.

FRANCES lifts a foot imperiously.

FRANCES: You do it.

Beat, OWEN puts his hands in his pockets, unwilling to touch FRANCES' foot.

FRANCES puts her foot down.

You knew how much I would hate this. All this. Seeing you pretending to be someone else.

OWEN: You came, though. You agreed.

FRANCES: Well, of course I agreed. But you knew how much I would hate it and you didn't even talk to me or look at me. Not once.

Pause.

OWEN kneels, lifts FRANCES' foot and takes off her shoes, rubs her feet.

She doesn't look anything like me. Or act, or speak or behave like me. Or think like me. Dress like me. We have nothing in common. We're completely unalike in everything. Totally and absolutely different. Was that a deliberate choice?

OWEN: It was nothing to do with choice. Nothing to do with you. She's who I fell in love with. And I do love her. I do.

FRANCES: Owen. These people will kill you. They're hateful. They'll kill you. You're different now. What are you going to be like in a few months, a few years time?

OWEN: I'll be fine.

FRANCES: Why have you done this, O?

OWEN: Because I'm at the age. And it's time to settle. Put down some roots. And I love her.

FRANCES suddenly slaps OWEN round the head. He barely reacts.

Pause.

Because I needed to do *something.*

Pause.

OWEN kneeling in front of FRANCES. He puts his face in her lap, pushes his hands up her skirt.

FRANCES: There's never been anyone else who even comes close. Not for me. It's only ever been you.

Since the beginning.

OWEN: I don't know what to do. Now. I don't know what to do.

FRANCES: Take your clothes off.

OWEN gets up and starts to undress.

FRANCES watches him.

Wait…

FRANCES goes to take off his wedding band. It's tight, so she puts his finger in her mouth. Pulls the ring off. Puts it to one side. Studies OWEN.

You're so beautiful. How can I do without you?

Music.

Light change.

Scene 2

Winter. Morning.

The kitchen of a large country house.

JULIA, a betrayed wife. KIERAN, a jack-of-all-trades. JULIA is on the phone. KIERAN has a large tube of sealant and a blow-torch.

JULIA: Liar! I know you know! Tell me! You tell me, you…you cow! Or I'll… He's my husband! I have a right –

Beat.

She hung up!

KIERAN: Julia?

JULIA re-dials.

Julia –

JULIA: So sorry to keep you waiting –

KIERAN: Should I leave? –

JULIA: Just one more little moment –

The other end is picked up.

You piss off!

She slams the phone down.

Hah! My sister-in-law. That'll show her.

KIERAN: Should I come back later?

JULIA: No.

KIERAN: I could do the leak –

JULIA: Forget the leak!

KIERAN: It'll spread.

JULIA: This house! Always something!

KIERAN: Do God knows how much damage. End up paying through the nose. I'll patch it up now.

JULIA: 'Patching'. I'm sick of it! I want something drastic! I want something done!

KIERAN: Give you some time. To get yourself together.

JULIA: No! No, no. Absolutely not. Phone call over. Moving on with my appointments. So. Where were we?

KIERAN: You said you wanted a quote?

JULIA: That's right. This wall. I want it gone.

KIERAN: What?

JULIA: Gone. I hate it. Get rid of it. I don't care what
it costs. Smash it! Rip it out! It's driving me crazy!
Just…get it out of here. I want to stand at the front
of the house and see all the way to the garden. I want
a clear view and I haven't got one so I want you
to do it. How much will it cost? Just to rip it down.
No, don't tell me. I don't care, just do it. Money no
object. Smash it.

KIERAN: This is a listed building.

JULIA: I'm so angry, I could kill.

KIERAN: That wall is five hundred years old.

JULIA: Take me against it.

KIERAN: Oh, God –

JULIA: Come on, it's history. You can have me up
against half a millennia of domestic structure.

KIERAN: I only had my breakfast this minute!

JULIA kisses KIERAN fiercely. Pulling at his clothes.
Bites his nipple.

Ow! Your teeth are bloody sharp!

JULIA: Exciting, isn't it? Turns you on, doesn't it?

KIERAN: It hurt!

JULIA pulls her knickers off under her skirt so that
they hang around one ankle. She arranges herself by
the wall.

JULIA: Punish me, then. Treat me like your whore. Use
me.

KIERAN: Why?

JULIA: I want you to. And stop asking bloody
    questions. All you've got to do is screw me. It's
    not that much to ask for. Crush my face into the
    500 hundred year old brick work. Push your blunt
    builder's fingers into me. Bruise me. Do me until
    I can't walk straight. And when you've finished, just
    leave. I want my thighs sticky with your dirty come.

KIERAN: You're way off beam, you are. What if I don't
    want to do it like that? What's wrong with going to
    bed? Being comfortable. I'm not a machine. I've got
    things on my mind too.

JULIA: Like what?

KIERAN: My mortgage. For starters.

JULIA: Christ's sake!

KIERAN: And all this urgency! You've got sod all else
    to do all day. What's the rush? What happened to
    long, slow kissing?

JULIA: I don't have the time.

KIERAN: I want a proper kiss.

    JULIA kisses KIERAN.

    He puts her hand on his crotch.

    See, wasn't so bad, was it?

JULIA: It was delightful. Now, get it out. We're going
    to have sex. And then you can go and see your
    mortgage broker. Or whoever it is you people
    deal with. And remember, I'm your bitch. You can
    do what you like with me. No explanations, no
    apologies. Let's go –

KIERAN: You've got some right front, you have.
Ordering people around.

JULIA: Good, I like it –

KIERAN: You think you're a proper fucking princess,
don't you?

JULIA: I do, yes –

KIERAN: You're no better than me –

JULIA: I'm getting really wet –

KIERAN: No, this isn't part of it.

JULIA: What?

KIERAN: I'm telling you something here. I'm sick of
the way you talk to me. So fucking arrogant. The
way you behave. Lady fucking Muck. Pisses me
off. You're not the boss of me. I don't have to do
everything you tell me –

JULIA: No, you don't but you usually do.

KIERAN: Well, I've had it.

JULIA: If you're just going to sulk –

KIERAN: No. We're going to redress the balance of this
a bit. We're going to do this differently.

JULIA: Why?

KIERAN: You said I could do what I liked with you. So,
I'm telling you what that is.

JULIA: Like what?

KIERAN: Something inventive. Erotic.

JULIA: Erotic.

KIERAN: Yeah. You know.

JULIA: Arouse me.

KIERAN: Alright then. You... (*Clears throat.*) You finger yourself. I watch.

JULIA: Ah.

KIERAN: Yeah?

JULIA: And you like the idea of that, do you?

KIERAN: Yeah, I do.

JULIA: To you, that constitutes the erotic.

KIERAN: Yeah, it 'constitutes' it alright. For me.

JULIA: You just can't be bothered!

KIERAN: I like it. It's a good idea. Dirty.

JULIA: I finger myself and you watch is erotic.

KIERAN: We can pretend I'm spying on you. Gives it an edge. The rough gamekeeper watching the lady of the manor bring herself off before he steps in to settle her hash with his brutal, meaty, proletarian cock. You like that sort of crap, don't you? Or perhaps you're just a bit shocked I know a word like proletarian.

JULIA: You lazy bastard!

Beat.

KIERAN: Are you shy? You're shy!

JULIA: No, I don't think I am.

KIERAN: You are. That's so sweet. Bashful Julesie –

JULIA: Don't call me that!

KIERAN: No point you being shy in front of me.

JULIA: I'm not shy!

KIERAN: Everyone does it, you know –

JULIA: I know.

KIERAN: You'll enjoy it. It's beautiful. It's natural to touch yourself.

JULIA: Kieran, I spend more time with my fingers wedged in my twat than you can possibly imagine.

KIERAN: Well, then. What's your problem –

JULIA: My problem is this. I'd be more than happy to sit over there and for your pleasure, 'finger' myself and enchanted as I am by that phrase, it's a pastel hued description of what you would actually see because, Kieran, although I make no secret of the fact that I hold you in pretty low esteem, even I would baulk at treating you to the sight of me strumming frantically in the futile hope of achieving even the faintest flicker of genuine excitement, a possibility so far away as to not even be remote! And I know that your regard for me is equally miserly but something in you might be moved by the expression of screwed and desperate concentration on my face, for take it from me, I am no gently moaning nymphet and the sight of all this anguish, this human suffering might compel you towards tenderness, to a sense of pity. You might try and kiss me with some level of compassion and that I could not bear. So. No. I am not going to sit over there and finger myself while you sit over here and watch.

KIERAN: You can't be bothered, can you.

JULIA: No. No, I can't. It's just another of those little jobs around the house that I pay you for. So, just get it done.

Pause.

KIERAN lights a cigarette. Waits.

He won't touch me. Hasn't ever. Not really. If I touch him, he…submits. He shuts his eyes so he doesn't have to look at my body. He doesn't like to be inside me. Not fingers, not tongue. Five hours after we were married, he'd lost the ring, said it went down the shower drain. He doesn't even like to come inside me.

KIERAN: You married a pouf. Plenty do.

JULIA: No. It's different. He was different. Something happened. There's someone else. I know it. He turns away from me. He makes me feel disgusting.

KIERAN: You are.

JULIA: If I was in a room full of other naked women and we all put a bag over our heads, he wouldn't be able to pick me out. I'm not special to him. If I was decapitated and lying on a slab, he wouldn't be able to identify me. He wouldn't know who I was. I am appalling to him. And who can I tell? No-one. Not a soul.

KIERAN: So why are you telling me?

JULIA: Because you don't count.

Beat.

KIERAN walks swiftly to JULIA, puts his hand roughly up her skirt, lifting her onto her toes.

JULIA grips his shoulders to steady herself.

KIERAN: This may come as some surprise to you, Julia, but things have really changed in the last hundred years. We get taught to read and write these days. We're even allowed to vote now! Perhaps you hadn't noticed?

Just as swiftly, KIERAN takes his hand away. Wipes his hand across her breasts. Walks back to his original position, carries on smoking. Pause.

JULIA: You're only a fucking handy-man, Kieran!

KIERAN: Yeah, aren't I just. All those little jobs around the house.

Pause.

KIERAN smokes.

JULIA: Don't make me beg.

Beat.

Don't make me beg you.

Pause.

Please.

KIERAN: That's more like it.

Music.

A light change.

Scene 3

Spring. Night.

FRANCES' living room.

FRANCES and RUSSELL, a failing media publishing executive. FRANCES wear a gold ring on a chain round her neck. They are having sex, an uncomfortable position.

RUSSELL: My arm –

FRANCES: What –

RUSSELL: Gone dead –

FRANCES: Shit –

She moves slightly.

RUSSELL: Better –

FRANCES: Harder –

RUSSELL: Oh –

FRANCES: That's it –

RUSSELL: Jesus –

FRANCES: That's it, there –

RUSSELL: Oh, Skin –

FRANCES: Getting there –

RUSSELL: Ah Skinner –

FRANCES: Nearly there – Now –

RUSSELL: Skinner –

FRANCES: What?

She stops.

He carries on.

RUSSELL: Skinner – Fucking bastard – You shit –

FRANCES: Russell! Russ –

RUSSELL: I've got to stop. I've got to stop now. It's a nightmare.

FRANCES: Do you know what you just said?

RUSSELL: I didn't say anything –

FRANCES: You said Skinner. You said Skinner's name!

RUSSELL: Jesus.

FRANCES: What the hell is going on in your head?

RUSSELL: Oh my God.

FRANCES: Clear your thoughts. You shouldn't be thinking about him. Not right now –

FRANCES starts to move again.

RUSSELL: No, stop. Stop a minute. I can't keep doing this.

FRANCES: With me?

RUSSELL: I can't concentrate. I can't get Skinner out of my head. It's not the face I want to see.

FRANCES: I can't believe you say his name!

RUSSELL: It's all gone fucking pear-shaped!

FRANCES: You don't want him here, do you?

RUSSELL: I don't want him anywhere! Frances, please, stop for a minute...just stop. For a minute. Please. Stop.

Pause.

FRANCES and RUSSELL still.

FRANCES: (*Together.*) Please don't start talking about yourself –

RUSSELL: I keep seeing the gloating bastard all the time – what?

FRANCES: Nothing, no, carry on, do –

RUSSELL: No, don't get off. Stay there. Please, just… stay –

FRANCES: Alright. Well?

RUSSELL: All the time, Skinner. On my back at work. All the time. There's no let-up. And he's everywhere! It's like I've been possessed! There's no escape! When I'm trying to have a shit, when I'm trying to sleep, when I'm fucking, especially when I'm fucking. I get this image of him standing over me, jiggling his balls, saying 'Call that an emission?' and then a great biblical flood of Skinner's semen comes gushing out of his trousers. All over my desk, clogging up my keyboard, all over my work, dripping into my phone, over my trousers, into my shoes, it splashes into my eyes and it really fucking stings! And then he leans over me and says 'Now, *that's* an emission, Russell. A man's emission. Now get to work. You cunt.'

FRANCES: You're not in the office now. This is leisure time.

RUSSELL: When you were a kid, did you ever think 'I can't wait to be grown up. Have a flat, job. Live in the city. Fuck who I want, when I want, how I want.' Did you think that?

FRANCES: Probably. I don't remember.

RUSSELL: You must have done.

FRANCES: Like I say, I don't remember. It's not relevant.

RUSSELL: My Auntie Gillian caught me fiddling with myself once. My Dad's sister. All prim and proper she was. I was about five or six. Having my bath. Just inspecting my willy, flipping it about. She went completely garrety. Scrubbed at my dirty little hands with the nailbrush. Made me cry. 'Don't tear your ticket, the conductor will tell you off!' What was that supposed to mean?

FRANCES: Maybe she had a fetish for public transport.

RUSSELL: Tear your ticket. Fuck. Course, when I was teenage, trying to get into clubs and gigs and that, bouncers saying 'You gotta ticket? Show us your ticket' and I'm back with my auntie Gillian. Five years old, trying to play with my winkle and being scared that it would rip and I'd be thrown off the bus.

FRANCES: What bus?

RUSSELL: The bus. Any bus. *The bus.* This dream of being grown up. Life being one long shag-fest with quick re-fuelling stops for beer and fags.

FRANCES: You're only thirty-four, Russ.

RUSSELL: I know. I've got a flat. I've got a job. Just about. I've got money. I've got sex. I can have as much of it as I want, when I want, how I want and I don't want it.

FRANCES: (*Lighting a cigarette.*) What am I doing sitting on this, then?

RUSSELL: I've got wood. So what. Don't want that either. I don't know what to do with it.

FRANCES: It's why we're both here.

RUSSELL: I wish it would just go away. Is there anywhere you don't smoke?

FRANCES: When I'm asleep. Are we just going to stay like this? It seem a shame to waste it.

RUSSELL: See? It gets in the way.

FRANCES: In the way of what.

RUSSELL: Talking. Getting to know each other. Makes a mockery of it. Can't have a conversation with someone with a boner you could hang your hat on sticking out your trousers.

FRANCES: I thought we had an agreement, Russ –

RUSSELL: I know. I know but… Things change.

Beat.

FRANCES smokes.

FRANCES: Shall we get back to it?

RUSSELL touches the gold ring she wears round her neck on a chain.

RUSSELL: Whose is this?

FRANCES: It's mine.

RUSSELL: But whose was it?

FRANCES: Why do you want to know?

RUSSELL: I'm interested.

FRANCES gets off. Moves away.

Beat.

RUSSELL inspects his erection.

I mean, this isn't right. I think I might have some kind of medical condition. It's always rock solid! Engorged! I don't have any control over it! It's got it's own malign life force! No wonder I have hallucinations about Skinner! My brain's deprived of blood! It's all in this monster!

FRANCES: I can't believe that you're worried about it.

RUSSELL: Why would a grown woman do that to a little kid? Why would someone do that? Make a little kid cry? It's fucking evil, isn't it?

FRANCES: Russ, you can't keep looking over your shoulder.

RUSSELL: When I have kids, if they want to spend the whole day with their hands down the front of their trousers, they can. I'm not going to stop them, I'll encourage it. Rule Number One in my house. A good solid wank and *then* you can watch telly. That's the kind of father I'm going to be.

FRANCES: That's actually really frightening.

RUSSELL: I want them to grow up with a healthy attitude.

FRANCES: They won't if you're going to be the Pol Pot of masturbation. God almighty. I feel like calling Social Services now and warning them in advance –

RUSSELL: You could keep me in some sort of order. Stop me from going too far with the kids.

Beat.

FRANCES: What?

Beat.

Oh, no. I don't think so…

RUSSELL: Relax, it was only a joke.

FRANCES: It had better be.

RUSSELL moves to FRANCES, looks at the ring, puts the tip of his finger through it.

RUSSELL: Your dad's?

FRANCES: No.

RUSSELL: Your mum's.

FRANCES: No.

RUSSELL: No. She'd have to have had fingers like a fucking navvy's to wear that. Fits me.

FRANCES takes the ring away from RUSSELL, puts it inside her top. Hiding it.

So what about you?

FRANCES: What about me?

RUSSELL: You never say anything about yourself. Never talk about anything personal or about what you want or hope for…dreams or…anything!

FRANCES: Nothing to say.

RUSSELL: What about family?

Beat.

FRANCES: I don't have one.

RUSSELL: No-one?

Beat.

FRANCES: There was a disagreement. We're estranged. End of story.

RUSSELL: Pretty serious disagreement. Me and my family are always fighting but we still see each other.

FRANCES: Maybe you should give estrangement a go. It's very liberating.

RUSSELL: Why don't you just make it up? It can't have been that bad –

FRANCES: Russ, why are you pushing this –

RUSSELL: Because you never tell me anything!

FRANCES: Yeah, I'm keeping my side of the bargain!

RUSSELL: Fucking bargain, it's stupid! All this secrecy and not talking – Well, bollocks to it! We're spending time together, it's not international espionage! Jesus! You know, we do this and it's great. It really is. I don't know what I'd do, really, without it. I'd be so fucking lonely –

FRANCES: Shut up, stop it, you've gone too far –

RUSSELL: No, I'm going to finish. We have a... I think we have a connection. Together. We understand each other. It works. I'm not talking about work, I'm talking about us. It can't just be coincidence that we fit together like we do. I think there's something. And it's meant. We connect –

FRANCES: There's no such thing. Connections. It is a coincidence. There's no connection. Just anti-connections. It doesn't mean anything. We're just fucking, Russell. That's all it is.

RUSSELL: But it's not. I see you come. I know what your face looks like. I know what noise you make.

FRANCES: And I know what you look like and what sounds you make. Alright so, we're even.

RUSSELL: You put your finger up my arse.

FRANCES: Yes, I did. That doesn't make us kindred spirits.

RUSSELL: I don't even let a doctor do that without a struggle.

FRANCES: Look, Russ. We are uniquely blessed amongst all creatures that crawl between heaven and earth in that we have a variety of appendages and a variety of apertures and orifices and the imagination that allows us to experiment with what goes where and in what and that's great, it's terrific. Sometimes it's intensely pleasurable and sometimes only mildly so but please, don't interpret it for anything else. It is what it is. That's it. That's all.

RUSSELL: Not for me. I mean, I notice things. How you change.

FRANCES: I don't change.

RUSSELL: You do. You taste different. In your, you know, your cycle. I'm down there with my face in your cunt, Frances. I should know. Certain days, you have a kind of metallic sort of taste. Like copper. I think of this, when I watch you at work. That I know something about you that nobody else knows. I was watching you in that meeting the other day and you had a little frown on your face, just a little crease between your eyebrows, the same expression you have when my cock's in your mouth –

FRANCES: You're not supposed to be watching.

RUSSELL: I love that little crease. It moves me –

FRANCES: Whether I'm sucking your dick or at work, you're not supposed to be watching me –

RUSSELL: But I do. All the time. You know, we sit in the same rooms as each other, go to the same meetings, listen to the same bullshit, talk the same bullshit. We're probably going to lose our jobs on the same day –

FRANCES: I'm not going to lose my job –

RUSSELL: I walk past you in corridors and you don't even flicker, not even a sideways glance and I know you.

FRANCES: You don't.

RUSSELL: I know how your skin flushes. I know you've got a birthmark on the back of your thigh that looks like Pete Postlethwaite in profile. Counts for something. We sit at work and no-one knows. About us. And what we have. Everyone's going on about who's going to be out the door and did he jump or was he pushed and all I can think about is that some days your breasts...tits get swollen. The nipples are tender. You wince. There's a faint blue vein that runs across, it gets more pronounced. Closer to the surface of the skin. I think about that at work. It drives me crazy. I don't do a bloody stroke all day. If that bastard Skinner knew just how little I do, he'd throttle me. I deserve to get the sack. All I think about is that little blue vein and the pulse underneath it. But I'm more gentle then. Do you notice? Are you aware that I notice?

FRANCES: No.

RUSSELL: I just think it's a waste. To know each other this well, to be this intimate and not...develop it –

FRANCES: Russ, this isn't intimacy. It's forensic science!

RUSSELL: Alright but it's a start, isn't it?

Beat.

FRANCES: A start to what?

RUSSELL: You and me. I want to do girlfriend-boyfriend stuff. You know. Go out in public. I'd like that. Go to the pictures. Go on the London Eye and snog all the way round. Have a dirty weekend in Blackpool and go on a roller coaster. Go up the river on a boat. Stay over at night. Talk to you in the bath. Tell stupid jokes. Rub your back when you get period pains. Watch you sleep. What the fuck, what ever. Go on holiday.

FRANCES: Go up the North Circular to IKEA. Buy bookshelves.

RUSSELL: It's an idea. Why not? We can't stay like this for ever.

FRANCES: What's wrong with it?

RUSSELL: I think we could make this work. Between us.

FRANCES: There isn't any us.

RUSSELL: Right. I make this declaration but you don't want to know.

FRANCES: I can't.

RUSSELL: Is this what it's going to be for the rest of your life?

FRANCES: What do you mean?

RUSSELL: I hear the other's talk. This is why I want to be public. Shut them the fuck up. But you lay down the law that everything has to be private, all this cloak and dagger shit –

FRANCES: What talk?

RUSSELL: The other guys. From the sound of it, you must have had most of them at one time or another –

FRANCES: I have.

Beat.

RUSSELL: Well. I'm not exactly Mr Discerning. Used to be a time when all some girl had to do was just smile at me and I'd fall in love, and in my head, we'd already be married and made for each other. Before we'd even spoken, I'd have played out this whole fantasy of me coming in from work, her and the kids all coming to see me at the door, full of smiles. 'Daddy's home!' Of course, by the time we'd had a quick shaft round the back, we'd already got divorced and she'd taken the kids and all my money and moved in with her personal trainer. Can't remember the names or the faces of most of them. Don't even remember their bodies. Just rooms, furniture. The colour of the sheets. So I'm not passing judgement. I just don't like hearing them talk.

FRANCES: What do they say?

RUSSELL: That you're cold.

Beat.

FRANCES: I am.

RUSSELL: You can't live like this, Frances. It's a… desolating way to live. I should know. I was Grand Master of the squalid, meaningless fuck. No-one can do it.

FRANCES: I can.

Beat.

RUSSELL: Well, anyway. I wanted to tell you something about me. You don't have to tell me anything back. I wanted to tell you. So you had a better idea of who I was. It was just something that happened to me in my past. To someone else, it's nothing but it's stuck with me and you know, when people say 'What event shaped you?' That was the one for me. That shaped me.

FRANCES: It's in the past. You got over it.

RUSSELL: I don't know. I think I'm fucked up. I think I'm fucked up and I think I've fucked up.

FRANCES: It was your primary sexual experience. I think you're fucked up on your Auntie Gillian.

Beat.

RUSSELL: You're a nasty bitch, really, aren't you?

FRANCES: You have no idea.

RUSSELL: Do I embarrass you? Is that why you don't want anyone to know? Are you ashamed to be seen with me?

FRANCES: Yes.

RUSSELL: Right. Well. That told me, didn't it. So now what. Do we carry on? Like you said. Shame to waste it. It's still good for it. You could hit it with a hammer and it would still be good for it. Shall we get back to business?

FRANCES: I don't know.

RUSSELL: Do you want to come?

Beat.

FRANCES: Do you want to come?

RUSSELL: I think I want to go.

Music.

Light change.

Scene 4

Summer. Very early morning.

An anonymous room.

OWEN and ELERI, an assistant sports shop manager. OWEN wears a light summer suit. (The suit that was on a hanger in the hotel bedroom). ELERI wears a dressing gown. She looks a lot like FRANCES.

OWEN: This suit crumples the minute I put it on. Cost a fortune. Cost more than most people earn in a month and it still looks like I slept in it. There should be an etiquette book, really shouldn't there? Some kind of guide to how to behave in these situations. What might be appropriate. It's always very difficult, isn't it? Not that I make a habit of it. I haven't really done this before. This kind of spontaneous, anonymous... So I don't know what to say. How to behave. It's just when I saw you, I knew I had to come home with you. I didn't mean to pass out afterwards. I was going to leave. Not that I had a plan, like I say it was spontaneous, the only thought in my mind was that you were, are, extraordinary but after a decent interval, I was going to go. But it was like I'd been... pole-axed. And I think I might have been rough. With you. And I'm sorry because that isn't fair. And I didn't intend for it to be that way. I would have liked it to be sweet and tender and for you to enjoy yourself. But it's been a while. A long while. For me. Which I'm sure you could tell. And you probably didn't get too much out of it. Because, if I'm honest, I know I was rough. I know I was. And it's nothing to do with you. It's just that you look so like someone. So like her. I know you're not her, I mean I do remember. You're Eleri? See, I do remember. A nice name. Welsh. Although that might not be what I called you during...and I apologise for that. And you work in a sports shop. I do remember that much. But in a certain light, you do look like her and I got this kind of madness- A desperate, greedy madness. And I feel bad. Because I'm not that kind of man. The sort of man who uses women. I mean, I'm married. Which is why I was going to get a mini cab and go because obviously this is it and it can't happen again but I'm sure you understand that and after last night, you probably don't want to see me again and it's just as well because I am married. And you look like someone who knows their way around, has done this before. Not that I mean to suggest that you're as...a slut or anything but that you have a sophisticated understanding of the vagaries and inadequacies of...humanity. But I passed out in your bed. And here we are. In this situation. Oh, God but you are like her. An attitude. A way of standing. The way your hair falls over your eyes…

OWEN reaches out to brush ELERI's fringe away.

She flinches, slightly.

Beat.

So like her. I'm sorry for anything I might have said. Any names I might have called you. I hope I didn't hurt you. Physically. But if I did, I really didn't mean it. But you are so like her and…it was as if everything narrowed down to one single point and I lost myself. There was a white flash in my head, like a bulb blowing. Or something. And then I passed out. So I wasn't being rough with you because it was you. Just put it down to a temporary blind madness. Anyway. Goodbye.

ELERI comes to a decision.

ELERI: I found a lump.

OWEN: Well, that's terrible. You should call a friend. A good friend to be with you. Not a stranger. What can I do? I'd let you make a call from my mobile but the battery's down and anyway, obviously, you have a landline but I don't know what you expect me to be able to do or say about this? We don't know each other, I can't offer you anything. I have nothing to give you at all. Call a friend and I would wait with you until that friend arrives whoever she or…he may be but I meant to leave ages ago, just to get out and away and I would have done if I hadn't passed out and I'm already late and expected elsewhere. So, I'm sure everything will be alright and you'll be fine but there's no point asking me for any help or comfort –

ELERI: (*Gently.*) On you.

> *Silence. ELERI unzips OWEN's flies, puts her hand inside and feels. Takes his hand and guides it to the spot.*

> *OWEN feels what she has felt.*

> *ELERI moves away.*

> *OWEN re-zips his flies.*

> *Long pause.*

> Sorry.

> *Music.*

> *Light change.*

Scene 5

Autumn. Night.

A bar.

LORRAINE, a consultant oncologist and SKINNER a corporate reptile. LORRAINE is reading a book. Has a drink. SKINNER approaches with a drink. Sits. LORRAINE reads.

SKINNER: Hi.

> *LORRAINE looks briefly up from her book. Maybe she looks over her shoulder to see if SKINNER is talking to someone else.*

LORRAINE: Hi.

SKINNER: It's a bit quieter this end, isn't it?

LORRAINE: It was.

SKINNER: It's crazy back there. A real Saturday night atmosphere.

LORRAINE: Really.

SKINNER: Believe it. There's a whole lot of hormones back there. Place is awash. Had to get out.

LORRAINE: Right.

LORRAINE turns a page of her book. Sips her drink. Time passes.

SKINNER: It's not even Saturday.

LORRAINE: I'm sorry?

SKINNER: I said, it's not even Saturday. It's Wednesday.

LORRAINE: Yes, I know.

SKINNER: And yet it's a real Saturday night atmosphere. Back there. Not out here, though. Thank God. It's calmer. An oasis.

LORRAINE: That's why I sit here.

SKINNER: Something will kick off in there. It's volatile. There'll be tears before bedtime through there, I can tell you. You can be sure of that. Hair pulling. Scratching. Before too long, a full on bitch fight. You mark my words.

LORRAINE: I'll do that.

SKINNER: You hear people talk about testosterone.

LORRAINE: You do?

SKINNER: Yeah. Aggression, violence, destructive acts…

LORRAINE: ...pattern baldness...

SKINNER: ...men in groups, all barbaric rituals, spore spraying, territory marking. But through there, in the back bar? Oestrogen. There's going to be all sorts of trouble kicking off in there and it's only mid-week. There's enough oestrogen in that back bar to wax your hair.

Pause.

What are you reading?

LORRAINE shows him the cover of the book.

Oh, yes, the old...yeah, the old guy there. He knows what's what. What a writer. What a wordsmith.

LORRAINE: Have you've read this?

SKINNER: Yes. Sort of. Not exactly. I know people who have read it. So. No. I haven't. Read that book. But. I do watch Newsnight Review.

LORRAINE: Well, it's very good.

SKINNER: So they say. So I've heard. He certainly liked it.

LORRAINE: Who?

SKINNER: The one who never likes anything, the one who... I think he's Irish. I don't know what he does for a living, apart from being on Newsnight Review. But I'm pretty sure he's an Irishman. He's got that brogue.

LORRAINE: Tom Paulin.

SKINNER: That's the bloke. You watch it too. Things in common. I like it. Good omen.

LORRAINE: He's a poet.

SKINNER: Is he now. Well. If he can turn a living at that he must be pretty sharp.

LORRAINE: And a critic.

SKINNER: There we are. That's how he supplements his income. He's got to spend a lot of his working day engaged in active thought, hasn't he? No let up for him.

LORRAINE: I suppose not.

LORRAINE gets out a cigarette.

SKINNER: Here, let me...

LORRAINE: Thanks...

SKINNER lights LORRAINE's cigarette.

SKINNER: You don't mind me talking to you? Just sitting down and talking to you?

LORRAINE: No, that's fine.

SKINNER: I thought I should ask. Because say if you do and I'll –

LORRAINE: No, it's fine.

SKINNER: It's just that I was in that mayhem back there and everyone was, you know, screaming and shouting and laughing too hard at each other's jokes and I just thought to myself... 'I've got to get out of here! This is no fucking good!' And I fought my way out and saw you sitting there, with your book, looking at peace.

LORRAINE: I looked at peace?

SKINNER: Yes, you did. Just very quiet, with your book and your drink and you looked really good –

LORRAINE: Thank you.

SKINNER: – so I thought I'd come over and talk to you. I'm Skinner, by the way.

LORRAINE: Venetia.

Beat.

SKINNER: Venetia?

LORRAINE: That's right.

SKINNER laughs.

What's so funny?

SKINNER: I'm sorry. I just thought of blinds.

LORRAINE: Well, there we are. Some people think of Venice. Others think of blinds.

SKINNER: Sorry.

LORRAINE: No, don't apologise.

SKINNER: Perhaps you have one of those little…you know, pulleys that you can adjust –

LORRAINE: Excuse me?

SKINNER: – for the slats of the blinds, to let more sun in?

LORRAINE: I don't.

SKINNER: No. Venetia! It's a very beautiful name. So, Venetia, what do you do for a living?

LORRAINE: I'm an executive for a media publishing company.

SKINNER: No! Venetia, you're not going to believe this but so am I!

LORRAINE: Really.

SKINNER: Venetia, really. I really am. What a coincidence. Which company do you work for, Venetia?

LORRAINE: I'd really rather not talk about work if you don't mind.

SKINNER: Okay, just thought we could interface on some market strategies –

LORRAINE: I work all day. I don't want to think about it in my leisure hours.

SKINNER: That's fine with me, Venetia. It is, really. The last thing anyone wants to do is talk about bloody work when they're trying to relax. And yet, that is all that people do. Don't you find that, Venetia?

LORRAINE: Occasionally, yes –

SKINNER: You come out for a drink and before you know it, the conversation is all bitching and who's in, who's out, who got share options and who got the sack, who's fucking who... It eats away at your soul, Venetia.

LORRAINE: That's why I bring a book.

SKINNER: I don't blame you, Venetia. I really don't. Everyone needs a little bit of escapism. I had to sack someone today. Had to let her go. Grown woman. You'd expect her to take it on the chin. You know what she did? Spat at me. Hawked it out of her throat like a thug, like a fucking yob on the terraces and let fly. At me. Disgusting. But you, Venetia, create your own little oasis of tranquillity. You seem to me like a very serene person.

LORRAINE: Do I?

SKINNER: You do. Like a lake.

LORRAINE: A lake?

SKINNER: Absolutely, Venetia. Picture it. A lake surrounded by willows, a breeze ruffles the surface, making the sunlight dance and dazzle. There are bulrushes at the banks and dragonflies zip about. There are swans swimming together, dipping their beaks into the water, their graceful necks bending and arching. Like a ballet. In the woods, there are cuckoos and other songbirds. You lie by the lake, under the shade of one of the...mighty oaks. Your head pillowed at its root. There is the faint rustling of the leaves in the warm breeze, the dappled sunlight plays across your face. Hush! Listen... We hear the lyrical call of a grebe.

Pause.

LORRAINE: I'm a lake.

SKINNER: It's a good thing to be. At one with nature. Maybe I was thinking of Venice, because of your name, the sun on the water. But a lake comes more to mind because you can get really ripped off in foreign cities and when I look at you, I don't see stress, Venetia. I see harmony. It's the landscape of your karma.

LORRAINE: And what about you.

SKINNER: I've really no idea. The landscape of my karma is probably slash-and-burn but I don't want to talk about me, Venetia. I want to talk about you.

LORRAINE: Okay. So...

SKINNER: So. Do you come here often?

Pause.

LORRAINE: Oh, fuck off!

SKINNER: What?

LORRAINE: When are you going to get to the point!

SKINNER: Don't blame me!

LORRAINE: I'm growing old and dying here!

SKINNER: You put me off.

LORRAINE: How? How did I put you off?

SKINNER: You said that thing about pattern baldness.

LORRAINE: When?

SKINNER: Right at the beginning. I was really getting into my stride and you said something about pattern baldness and it threw me off.

LORRAINE: A tiny throwaway comment –

SKINNER: I'm sensitive about it and you know it –

LORRAINE: You're not even trying! When it was my turn, I really worked hard at it. I surprised you when it was my turn, I was effective and the way you're going about it, I'd rather be reading my book! A fucking lake?

SKINNER: It's one of the first principles of extempore, sweet pants. Go with it.

LORRAINE: You didn't know where you were going with it –

SKINNER: Yes, I did –

LORRAINE: And that stuff about the spitting?

SKINNER: It really happened!

LORRAINE: What a show stopper of an anecdote that was! That really had me sliding off the seat!

SKINNER: That's my working day! Firing people and having them spit at me –

LORRAINE: Can we stop talking about this now, please?

SKINNER: It can't have come as that much of a surprise, she knew it was on the cards, she was the one who worked it all out. She went for me with her nails. Spat a great fat lump at me. Only just missed me. Landed on my desk. Big as an oyster. Crazy fucking cow. Security had to come and remove her. She went demented. Can I catch anything from that?

LORRAINE: T.B.

SKINNER: Bloody hell.

LORRAINE: But it's unlikely. And are we ever going to graduate to the point where you don't introduce yourself by your surname?

SKINNER: Nah. I don't like being called by my first name. Makes me uncomfortable. Jumpy.

LORRAINE: I'm having sex with a neurotic freak. Fuck my luck.

SKINNER: I'm not neurotic.

LORRAINE: Even the kids think you're weird.

SKINNER: I thought they liked me?

LORRAINE: They think you're strange.

SKINNER: I took them to fucking Bird World, trying to get them to like me. I got pecked by a fucking toucan.

LORRAINE: When it's my turn, I make an effort. I'm direct.

SKINNER: More than one way to skin a cat, love. I had my theory.

LORRAINE: And?

SKINNER: I was going to make contact. A bit of chat. Nothing too much. Some lingering eye meets, a hint of connection and then I was going to go –

LORRAINE: What!

SKINNER: And then I was going to come back, as you were leaving and come up really close to you, really close but not touching, so there was a real frisson of sexual electricity and then I was going to say something harsh and urgent in your ear…

LORRAINE: Like what?

SKINNER: Well, you're not going to know now, are you? You fucking ruined it. I mean, Venetia? Christ, Lorraine! That one really addled me –

LORRAINE: It's a name. I thought it was pretty. I thought it would be different.

SKINNER: Venetia the media publishing executive! Why don't you just say what you do? You don't have to create a whole new persona –

LORRAINE: Because telling people you're an oncologist is like having a running sore on your face! Cancer is not a conversation starter. Either everyone avoids you or if they don't, they just want to talk about death and disease and rot –

SKINNER: Venetia! You dozy mare!

LORRAINE: Don't keep going on about it.

SKINNER: You always think you're the only one who's got any ideas about how to do this and you block me. I was building up a story here. You tore that apart.

LORRAINE: I didn't know where it was going.

SKINNER: It's my turn. It's not for you to know.

LORRAINE: Well, mea culpa, alright but if you want to know the truth, it wasn't working. Not for me.

Pause.

SKINNER: You got a new blouse?

LORRAINE: Blouse? Who am I? Your bloody granny?

SKINNER: Alright, shirt, top, 'tricot'. I don't know, do I? En-fucking-semble.

LORRAINE: Yes.

SKINNER: Looks alright. Suits you.

LORRAINE: Thank you.

Beat.

SKINNER checks his watch.

SKINNER: It's nearly closing.

LORRAINE: Shit. The babysitter wants double after midnight.

SKINNER: Shall we get another in?

LORRAINE: No, we'll have a drink at mine. Just...cut to the fucking chase, alright?

SKINNER: You still want to do this?

LORRAINE: Skinner, I've got a young guy in at the moment with a lump in his balls the size of an egg. A young man, younger than you. It's voracious. And I'll do my best but most of that will be damage limitation and after that it's just guesswork. My point being that while we sit here, we really are growing old and dying. This has got to feel like destiny. Like fate, like there is nothing else for us to do! Walking away from each other is not an option! Before we die, before our bodies betray us, we have to fuck each other. Because we've got all our feral miraculous senses. Because we love and feel passion and desire rocks us! Because we've got teeth and tongues and our hearts beat!

SKINNER: Jesus –

LORRAINE: Because we're alive. Here. Now. On the turning world. And we won't always be.

SKINNER: Alright.

LORRAINE: So enough with the preamble! Be direct! Predatory!

SKINNER: Alright!

LORRAINE: Make it matter! Surprise me!

SKINNER: Anything else?

LORRAINE: We're animals!

SKINNER: Alright! Bloody hell!

SKINNER leaves. Returns. Picks up his drink and takes it away with him.

LORRAINE goes back to her book. In the background, we see SKINNER talking to himself, perhaps playing out a little scenario, trying out phrases. He looks at LORRAINE reading. Something in the way he looks at her changes, he sees her differently. He approaches, stands a little way off. Watches LORRAINE.

She notices him.

SKINNER comes closer. Takes her book and puts it down on the bar.

LORRAINE: Hi...

Beat.

SKINNER still. Then he kisses LORRAINE, tenderly, deeply. A lover's kiss. The kiss lasts some time.

They move apart from each other.

Pause.

LORRAINE: I'll get my coat.

Music.

Lighting change.

Scene 6

Summer.

A hotel bedroom. Distantly, a party. As in Scene 1, although it is half an hour later.

FRANCES half-dressed in her bridesmaid dress is sitting on the bed. The phone is ringing. From off-stage, we hear the sound of water running. There is a half bottle of champagne from the mini-bar. The ring should be nearby, in a hotel ashtray, perhaps. FRANCES lights a cigarette. Off-stage the water is turned off. OWEN enters. He is wearing the light summer suit.

OWEN: How long's that been ringing?

Answers the phone.

Hello – Yes, I'm there – Just freshening up – Okay, she's here –

Holds the phone out.

She wants to talk to you.

FRANCES tries to take the receiver but OWEN keeps hold of it.

FRANCES: Hello? Yes, he's ready – Well, that's why I'm here – No, thank you – That would be lovely –Bye – Oh – and do thank your mother for me. So kind. So charming. Really made me feel welcome –

OWEN takes the phone away from her.

OWEN: I'll be a few moments – Yes – I can't wait either –

Phone goes down.

You should have answered it.

FRANCES: You don't trust me to hold the receiver but you think I should have answered it?

OWEN: She said it was ringing for ages. Fuck knows what they'll think.

FRANCES: They won't think anything. They have no cognitive ability. Anyway, what could be more touching? More natural?

OWEN sits. Puts on socks. Shoes.

'Freshening up.' You sound like an air hostess.

OWEN: For someone so actively engaged in class warfare, you're a real fucking snob.

FRANCES: I'm not a snob. I've got nothing against air hostesses. I just despise anyone who's never worked for a living. Who doesn't know the value of a quid. And so did you, once upon a time.

OWEN: Once.

FRANCES: And I'd hardly call that freshening up. You scrubbed. A very thorough scrubbing. Get every trace of me off you.

OWEN: You should wash.

FRANCES: I don't want to.

OWEN: You should. You reek of it. This whole room reeks of it.

FRANCES: Good. I won't be washing.

OWEN: They'll all be able to smell it on you.

FRANCES: I won't be coming down.

OWEN: Where are you going?

FRANCES: Home. That's it, now. I can't do anymore. I'm not that hard.

OWEN is ready.

Well, look at you.

OWEN: We can still see each other. Perhaps. It might be possible?

FRANCES: No.

OWEN: I mean, later. A few years?

FRANCES: This is it. It has the right air of doomed finality, doesn't it?

OWEN: What do I say to them?

FRANCES: Say we had a disagreement. Tell them we're estranged. End of story.

Beat.

OWEN: I have to go.

FRANCES: Does she want kids? I bet you she wants kids. One of each.

OWEN: Christ, I hope not. Might end up like us.

FRANCES: Go on. Go. Just fuck off.

OWEN gets up. They face each other. He reaches out and brushes hair out of her eyes.

She catches his hand, hold it against her face.

Your face breaks my heart.

OWEN: What will you do?

FRANCES: Carry on. Keep going. That's the fucking tragedy of it. No revelation. No epiphany. Just carrying on. And the world gone grey and merely ordinary.

OWEN: We'll be alright.

FRANCES: You're such a coward, Owen. You even cleaned your teeth.

Beat.

OWEN turns to go.

FRANCES picks up the ring from the side and holds it up in the air.

OWEN pauses, feels his hand.

OWEN: Shit…

Walks to FRANCES with his hand held out for the ring.

She puts it in her mouth, lifts the champagne.

FRANCES: To us.

Drinks and swallows.

All the major food groups.

OWEN: I'm not even surprised by that. I'll think of something. Between here and the marquee, I'll think of something. I'll probably say it was all your fault.

FRANCES: It is.

OWEN turns to go.

You'll miss me.

OWEN: I know.

The End.